Vladimir Putin's Background

When Vladimir Putin was appointed as prime minister of Russia, very little was known about his background. This former Soviet intelligence agent entered politics in the early 1990s and rose rapidly. By August of 1999, ailing President Boris Yeltsin (1931–) appointed him prime minister. When Yeltsin stepped down in December of 1999, Putin became the acting President of Russia, and he was elected President to serve a full term on March 26, 2000.

Early life and education

Vladimir Putin was born on October 1, 1952, in Leningrad (now St. Petersburg), Russia. An only child, the his father was a foreman in a metal factory, and his mother was a homemaker. Putin lived with his parents in an apartment with two other families. Though religion was not permitted in the Soviet Union, the former country which was made up of Russia and other smaller states, his mother secretly had him baptized as an Orthodox Christian.

Though a small child, Putin could hold his own in fights thanks to martial arts classes. By the age of sixteen, he was a top-ranked expert at sambo, a Russian combination of judo and wrestling. By the time he was a teenager, Putin had begun to display the ambition that he later became known for and he attended a respected high school, School 281, which only accepted students with near-perfect grades. The institution was the only one in Russia to stress chemistry, which was Putin's interest. However, he soon moved toward liberal arts and biology. Putin played handball and worked at the school radio station, where he played music by the Beatles and other Western rock bands. Fascinated with spy movies as a teen, he aspired to work for the KGB, the Russian secret service.

Work in the KGB

At Leningrad State University, Putin graduated from the law department in 1975, but instead of entering the law field right out of school, Putin landed a job with the KGB, the only one in his class of one hundred to be chose. The branch he was assigned to was responsible for recruiting foreigners who would work to gather information for KGB intelligence.

In the early 1980s, Putin met and married his wife, Lyudmila, a former teacher of French and English. In 1985 the KGB sent him to Dresden, East Germany, where he lived undercover as Mr Adamov, the Director of the Soviet-German House of Friendship, a social and cultural club. Putin appeared to genuinely enjoy spending time with Germans, unlike many other KGB agents and respected the German culture.

Around the time Putin went to East Germany, Soviet leader Mikhail Gorbachev (1931–) was beginning to introduce economic and social reforms (improvements). Putin was apparently a firm believer in the changes. In 1989 the Berlin Wall, which stood for nearly forty years separating East from West Germany, was torn down, and the two united. Though Putin supposedly had known that this was going to happen, he was disappointed that it occurred amid chaos and that the Soviet leadership had not managed it better.

Russian politics

In 1990 Putin returned to Leningrad and continued his undercover intelligence work for the KGB. In 1991, just as the Soviet Union was beginning to fall apart, Putin left the KGB with the rank of colonel in order to get involved in politics. Putin went to work for Anatoly Sobchak, the mayor of St. Petersburg, as an aide and, in 1994, became deputy mayor.

During Putin's time in city government, he reportedly helped the city build highways, telecommunications, and hotels, all to support foreign investment. Although St. Petersburg never grew to become the financial powerhouse that many had hoped, its fortunes improved as many foreign investors moved in, such as Coca-Cola and Japanese electronics firm NEC.

On to the Kremlin

In 1996, when Sobchak lost his mayoral campaign, Putin was offered a job with the victor but declined out of loyalty. The next year, he was asked to join President Boris Yeltsin's "inner circle" as deputy chief administrator of the Kremlin, the building that houses the Russian government. In March 1999, he was named secretary of the Security Council, a body that advises the President on matters of foreign policy, national security, and military and law enforcement.

In August of 1999, after Yeltsin had gone through five prime ministers in seventeen months, he appointed Putin, who many thoughts were not worthy of succeeding the ill President. For one thing, he had little political experience; for another, his appearance and personality seemed boring. However, Putin increased his appeal among citizens for his role in pursuing the war in Chechnya. In addition to blaming various bombings in Moscow and elsewhere on Chechen terrorists, he also used harsh words in criticizing his enemies. Soon, Putin's popularity ratings began to soar.

Acting President of Russia

In December 1999, Russia held elections for the 450-seat Duma, the lower house of Russia's parliament (governing body). Putin's newly-formed Unity Party came in a close second to the Communists in a stunning showing. Though Putin was not a candidate in this election, he became the obvious front-runner in the upcoming presidential race scheduled for June of 2000.

On New Year's Eve in 1999, Yeltsin unexpectedly stepped down as President, naming Putin as acting President. Immediately, Western news media and the U.S. government scrambled to create a profile of the new Russian leader. Due to Putin's secretive background as a KGB agent, there was little information. His history as a spy caused many Westerners and some Russians as well to question whether he should be feared as an enemy of the free world.

In Putin's first speech as acting President, he promised, "Freedom of speech, freedom of conscience, freedom of the press, the right to private property—these basic principles of a civilized society will be protected," according to a Newsweek report. In addition, Putin removed several of Yeltsin's loyalists and relatives from his cabinet.

Elected President

On March 26, 2000, Russians elected Putin out of a field of eleven candidates. After his election, Putin's first legislative move was to win approval of the Start II arms reduction treaty from the Duma. The deal, which was negotiated seven years earlier, involved decreasing both the Russian and American nuclear buildup by half. Putin's move on this issue was seen as a positive step in his willingness to develop a better relationship with the United States. In addition, one of the Putin's earliest moves involved working with a team of economists to develop a plan to improve the country's economy. On May 7, 2000, Putin was officially sworn in as Russia's second president and the first in a free transfer of power in the nation's eleven-hundred-year history.

Putin, a soft-spoken and stone-faced man keep his personal life very private. In early 2000, an American publishing company announced that in May, it would release an English-language translation of his memoirs, First Person, which was banned from publication in Russia until after the March 26 presidential election.

Putin has made great efforts to improve relations with the remaining world powers. In July 2001, Putin met with Chinese President Jiang Zemin (1926–), and the two signed a "friendship treaty" which called for improving trade between China and Russia and improving relations concerning the U.S. plans for a missile defence system. Four months later, Putin visited Washington, D.C., to meet with President George W. Bush (1946–) over the defence system. Although they failed to reach a definite agreement, the two leaders did agree to drastically cut the number of nuclear arms in each country. Early in 2002, Putin travelled to Poland and became the first Russian President since 1993 to make this trip. Representatives of the two countries signed agreements involving business, trade, and transportation.

Xi Jinping's Background

Xi Jinping (born June 15?, 1953, in Fuping county, Shaanxi province, China) is a Chinese politician and government official who served as vice president of the People's Republic of China (2008–13), general secretary of the Chinese Communist Party (CCP; 2012–), and President of China (2013–).

Early life

Xi Jinping was the son of Xi Zhongxun, who once served as deputy prime minister of China and was an early comrade-in-arms of Mao Zedong. The elder Xi, however, was often out of favour with his Party and government, especially before and during the Cultural Revolution (1966–76) and after he openly criticized the government's actions during the 1989 Tiananmen S□uare incident. The youngerXi's early childhood was largely spent in the relative luxury of the residential compound of China's ruling elite in Beijing. During the Cultural Revolution, however, with his father purged and out of favour, Xi Jinping was sent to the countryside in 1969 (he went to largely rural Shaanxi province), where he worked for six years as a manual labourer in an agricultural commune.

During that period, he developed an especially good relationship with the local peasantry, which would aid the wellbornXi's credibility in his eventual rise through the ranks of the CCP.

Entry into the CCP, education, and marriage

In 1974 Xi became an official party member, serving as a branch secretary, and the following year he began attending Beijing's Tsinghua University, where he studied chemical engineering. After graduating in 1979, he worked for three years as secretary to Geng Biao, who was then the vice premier and minister of national defence in the central Chinese government.

In 1982 Xi gave up that post, choosing instead to leave Beijing and work as a deputy secretary for the CCP in Hebei province. He was based there until 1985 when he was appointed a party committee member and a vice mayor of Xiamen (Amoy) in Fujian province. While living in Fujian, Xi married the well-known folksinger Peng Liyuan in 1987. He continued to work his way upward, and by 1995 he had ascended to the post of deputy provincial party secretary.

Ascension in the CCP

In 1999 Xi became acting governor of Fujian, and he became governor the following year. Among his concerns as Fujian's head were environmental conservation and cooperation with nearby

Taiwan. He held both the deputy secretarial and governing posts until 2002, when he was elevated yet again: that year marked his move to Zhejiang province, where he served as acting governor and, from 2003, party secretary. While there, he focused on restructuring the province's industrial infrastructure in order to promote sustainable development.

Xi's fortunes got another boost in early 2007 when a scandal surrounding the upper leadership of Shanghai led to his taking over as the city's party secretary. His predecessor in the position was among those who had been tainted by a wide-ranging pension fund scheme. In contrast to his reformist father, Xi had a reputation for prudence and for following the party line, and as Shanghai's secretary, his focus was squarely on promoting stability and rehabilitation of the city's financial image. He held the position for only a brief period. However, as he was selected in October 2007 as one of the nine members of the standing committee of the CPP's Political Bureau (Politburo), the highest ruling body in the Party.

With that promotion, Xi was put on a short list of likely successors to Hu Jintao, general secretary of the CCP since 2002 and President of the People's Republic since 2003. Xi's status became more assured when in March 2008, he was elected vice president of China. In that role, he focused on conservation efforts and on improving international relations. In October 2010, Xi was named vice chairman of the powerful Central Military Commission

(CMC), a post once held by Hu (who since 2004 had been chair of the commission) and generally considered a major stepping-stone to the presidency. In November 2012, during the theCCP's 18th party congress, Xi was again elected to the standing committee of the Political Bureau (reduced to seven members), and he succeeded Hu as general secretary of the Party. At that time, Hu also relinquished the chair of the CMC to Xi. On March 14, 2013, he was elected President of China by the National People's Congress.

Consolidation of power

Among's first initiatives was a nationwide anti-corruption campaign that soon saw the removal of thousands of high and low officials (both "tigers" and "flies"). Xi also emphasized the importance of the " rule of law, " calling for adherence to the Chinese constitution and greater professionalization of the judiciary as a means of developing "socialism with Chinese characteristics. "Under's leadership, China was increasingly assertive in international affairs, insisting upon its claim of territorial sovereignty over nearly all of the South China Sea despite an adverse ruling by the Permanent Court of Arbitration in The Hague and promoting its "One Belt, One Road" initiative for joint trade, infrastructure, and development projects with East Asian, Central Asian, and European countries.

Xi managed to consolidate power at a rapid pace during his first term as China's President. The success of his anti-corruption campaign continued, with more than one million corrupt officials, being punished by late 2017; the campaign also served to remove many ofXi's political rivals, further bolstering his efforts to eliminate dissent and strengthen his grip on power. In October 2016, the CCP bestowed upon him the title of "core leader, " which previously had been given only to influential party figures Mao Zedong, Deng Xiaoping, and Jiang Zemin; the title immediately raised his stature. A year later, the CCP voted to enshrine Xi's name and ideology, described as "thought" ("Xi Jinping Thought on Socialism with Chinese Characteristics in a New Era"), in the Party's constitution, an honour previously awarded only to Mao. Xi's ideology was later enshrined in the country's constitution by an amendment passed by the National People's Congress (NPC) in March 2018. During the same legislative session, the NPC also passed other amendments to the constitution, including one that abolished term limits for the country's President and vice president; this change would allow Xi to remain in office beyond 2023 when he would have been due to step down. The NPC also unanimously elected Xi to a second term as President of the country in March.

Xi's power and influence were bolstered in 2021 when the CCP passed a historical resolution in November that reviewed the Party's "major achievements and historical experience" of the past 100 years and looked to future plans as well. It featured praise for Xi's leadership; more than half of the document was devoted to the accomplishments under Xi in the nine years he had led the Party, such as reducing poverty and curbing corruption. It was only the third such resolution in the Party's history—the previous two were passed under Mao and Deng—and it elevatedXi's status, ensuring that he would be seen as a significant figure in the Party's history.

ARE VLADIMIR PUTIN AND XI JINPING TWO OF A KIND?

In many countries, individuals have taken all the power into their own hands. This is true, not least of Russia and China. Vladimir Putin has used his power to invade Ukraine. Recently, Xi Jinping practised encircling Taiwan.

Similarities Between Putin And Xi

Putin and Xi have good personal chemistry and a close strategic partnership. During the opening of the 2022 Winter Olympics in Beijing, they declared that their friendship was "limitless". They are the same age; both will soon be 70. Putin came to power in 1999, and Xi in 2012.

President Xi's first foreign trip was to Moscow, where he claimed that China and Russia's partnership was the world's most important bilateral relationship.

In order to remain in power, both men have rejected rules designed to limit their terms in office. Russia is due for a presidential election in 2024. In 2018, Putin said he would not stand. This seems scarcely credible. Xi will ensure that he is re-elected during the Chinese Communist Party's 20th Congress this November. Neither man has nurtured potential successors.

And both see themselves as facing the same enemies: the United States/NATO/the west/Japan. And both have the same deep fear: a western-supported democratic uprising.

They viewed the demonstrations in Kyiv in 2014 and in Hong Kong in 2014 and 2019 as being controlled from abroad. Accordingly, Putin and Xi both need systems to exert strong internal repression. In addition, they have the world's second-and third-largest military forces at their disposal. Russia has a large number of nuclear weapons. China has far fewer nuclear weapons but a larger number of more modern conventional armaments.

Both Putin and Xi nurse grievances about the humiliations suffered by their countries in the past. They see it as their mission to regain lost territories. The Russian Federation and the People's Republic of China are two continental empires. Each has a dominant ethnic group (Russians; Han Chinese) and a number of ethnic minorities. Minority groups in both countries suffer severe repression if they demand political self-government.

In the years 2001–2005, China and Russia entered into border pacts. They have worked together successfully through the Shanghai Cooperation Organisation, which encompasses all the Central Asian countries. The Soviet Union's internal borders formed the basis for those of its successor states after it collapsed in 1991, but since then, Putin has sought to redraw these borders by intervening in Georgia, annexing Crimea, and invading Ukraine.

For many years before Xi came to power, China had focused on negotiating secure borders. It was very successful. All of its land borders are agreed upon, apart from those with India and Bhutan. In contrast, China's maritime borders are highly controversial, and the Taiwan issue has become ever more deadlocked. Putin and Xi benefit from the security of their countries" borders in Central Asia, which has allowed them to focus on territorial expansion in the Black Sea and the western Pacific Ocean.

Differences Between Putin And Xi

Earlier in his career, Putin was an intelligence officer in the KGB, the forerunner of today's FSB. Xi rose through the ranks of the Chinese Communist Party.

Putin governs a corrupt "mafia state". His political Party, United Russia, has limited significance apart from ensuring that he gets re-elected. Xi governs a systemically constructed one-party state and has tightened the Communist Party's grip on government, business, schools, and universities.

Russia has an oil- and gas-based export economy, but its other industrial sectors are poorly developed. Exports account for over 25 per cent of Russia's gross domestic product (GDP). China is also heavily oriented towards exports (18 per cent of GDP), but China has a diversified industrial sector that is dependent on global production and marketing chains.

It is possible to be an opposition politician in Russia, although one will be persecuted and risk being murdered. In China, the opposition is pretty much impossible.

Both countries have a lot of corruption, but Xi has engaged in forceful anti-corruption efforts. Putin uses corruption as an instrument of internal power.

The oppression of political opposition in Russia is severe but somewhat haphazard. It is possible to be an opposition politician in Russia, although one will be persecuted and risk being murdered. In China, the opposition is pretty much impossible. The one-party state has become a digitized police state.

Putin And Xi Use Their Military Power In Different Ways.

Putin has engaged in active warfare in Chechnya, Georgia, Syria, and Ukraine and is expending more military resources than Russia can really afford. The Chinese economy is strong enough to finance a modern military sector. As a result, China'sPeople's Army has become far more powerful than Russia's. Despite this fact, China has not been at war since the 1980s. The clashes with India in 2020 in the Himalayas consisted of hand-to-hand fighting with makeshift weaponsChina'sPeople's Army lacks battle experience.

From an American perspective, China's military strength puts Russia in second place as a strategic threat. The primary threat is China because Xi's future prospects are much better than Putin's.

Russia is a declining power. China can expect to increase its power for another couple of decades.

Russia is a declining power. China can expect to increase its power for another couple of decades. At that point, demographics will become an issue. China's lower birth rate has caused the number of Chinese people of working age to stagnate; soon, the number will start to fall. This decline will make it difficult for China to assemble the forces necessary to mount a military challenge to the United States and its allies.

Some see this as comforting. Others fear that Xi will become more audacious as the prospects of continued Chinese growth weaken. Will he think that he has one last chance to conquer Taiwan?

This will depend on the ageingXi's state of mind. Will he become more like Putin?

Willingness to take risks is associated with paranoia, impulsivity, recklessness, and narcissism. Such personality traits seem more prominent in the Russian leader than in Xi. Xi appears to be methodical, calculating, and unscrupulous but also patient. He has generated a cult around himself and his ideas, but he presents himself as a highly effective bureaucrat.

Preventing war in East AsiaXi's bureaucratic and methodical approach gives hope that China will continue to avoid war with the United States as well as with its neighbours.

In practice, this means that China will have to live with the status quo as far as Taiwan is concerned. Even after the military exercises around Taiwan, the missiles that passed over Taiwan, and the Chinese fighter jets that crossed the median line of the Taiwan Strait, Taipei and Washington would do well to note the limits of's willingness to take risks.

The adoption of a consistent and pragmatic policy by the West can help maintain the status quo regarding Taiwan and prevent war in East Asia.

Why China's Xi Is Not "Putin-Plus."

Xi Jinping is not following in Vladimir Putin's footsteps. He's carving his own path.

The recently announced constitutional amendments in China, ending term limits and paving the way for Chinese leader Xi Jinping's indefinite rule, have sparked ?uite a lot of debate and speculation in Western media.

Some commentators went as far as comparing Xi to Russian President Vladimir Putin, claiming that China is now turning into a Russia-style autocracy. While the phrase "Putin-plus "sounds catchy, the comparison does not reflect the facts on the ground.

Xi's regime is indeed changing gears and starting on a more autocratic path, but Chinese governance practices are radically different from those in Russia. Lumping the two countries together into a vague category of "one-man dictatorship" distorts reality and doesn't help western audiences understand and engage with them.

The Chinese political system thus far still remains more institutionalized, more adaptive to public opinion, and more aspirational globally. When it comes to governance, both domestic and global, the Chinese form of authoritarianism is outperforming Russia's.

The Party And Chinese Public Opinion

Unlike Russia, China boasts a strong party, heavily integrated into all levels of Chinese society. From the media to entertainment to Western enterprises, the Chinese Communist Party (CCP) is a vast and powerful organization with over 80 million members, which directly and indirectly co-opts Chinese citizens into the political system. Its reach has extended from the media and entertainment industries all the way to foreign companies, where it has started planting its own units.

The CCP can be frustratingly opaque, but there has been some push for transparency from within. For example, last December, the "Open Party Regulations" – first proposed during the Hu Jintao presidency – were passed, signalling a renewed effort for more open access to information. These regulations allow party members and the general public to request and receive certain types of records, albeit with heavy constraints.

At the same time, despite increasing repression against activists and grassroots organizations, the regime has has still been open to institutionalized political participation by ordinary Chinese citizens. Under Xi, institutionalized channels for reporting grievances have been reinforced, allowing for a more controlled gathering of information on public opinion.

In contrast to state-society relations in Russia, which have been described by scholars and observers as a "no-participation pact " ", with citizens exchanging silence for stability, in the Chinese political system, the Party obsessively studies and responds to public opinion.

Apart from the increasingly institutionalized public feedback channels, we have witnessed an expansion of digital deliberation channels under Xi, with Chinese officials opening more pages on Weibo (the Chinese eＺuivalent of Twitter) to communicate with the general public. The regime has also launched new digital media outlets, like Pengpai (The Paper, which is owned by the Shanghai local government). While such outlets regularly offer rather fulsome praise of President Xi, they also often uncover corruption and expose governance failures across various institutions.

The Party increasingly does not see public support as a given. In some of his recent speeches on internet policy, Xi has described public opinion management as a "battlefield " ". That is, the regime has to "fight" for positive public opinion, using various channels to grasp public concerns and more sophisticated tools to persuade.

My research on journalists in China and Russia found that even in the domains of traditional media, Chinese authorities have been more responsive to journalistic investigations than their Russian counterparts. Interviews I did with critical media professionals in both countries revealed that, whereas Chinese journalists tend to get at least some reaction to their reports, often in the form of modest policy change, their Russian colleagues say they "can't reach the other side [the state]" at all.

There is a sense of co-participation in governance among China's journalists – a fluid, albeit now-tested partnership with the party-state. On the Russian side, there is more of a sense of exasperation and a tense cohabitation between media professionals and the state.

Thus, in China, the Party seeks legitimacy by drawing more heavily on societal feedback that is collected and studied through a variety of channels. In Russia, the regime relies heavily upon on Putin's popularity and on internal accountability checks through the "power vertical" rather than through horizontal public opinion surveying.

Personality Cults And International Aspirations

Putin and Xi have also approached building personality cults in different ways. For over a decade now, the Russian President has preferred to portray himself as a macho man, fearlessly tackling anything that comes his way, from saving tigers to standing up to Western aggression.

Xi, on the other hand, has adopted the image of a father figure. As a result, he is often referred to as "Big Daddy Xi" in the public arena. This portrayal was quite explicit in the recent CCTV propaganda film about the Chinese President called "A family nation under heaven."

Xi's personification of power has also been more tech-savvy than Putin's. The Chinese propaganda machine has created multiple apps dedicated to tracking Xi's travels, studying his speeches, and interpreting all his latest policies. By contrast, Putin's rule has been dotted with P.R. blunders, the latest one of which was the use of a 2007 video during his state-of-the-nation speech to illustrate a supposedly brand-new nuclear missile.

The two countries also operate differently in the international arena. Russia projects its strength mostly through aggression and political interference, while China is pursuing an intentional authoritarian governance model.

Xi's Belt and Road Initiative and his explicit support for globalization are strikingly different from Putin's strategy of launching military operations and engaging in subversive acts abroad (such as the alleged interference in the U.S. elections).

Xi's slogans, the "China Dream" and "Telling the China Story," speak of China's drive to propagate an alternative to the Western democratic model. Whether he will succeed in his ambition of symbolically and logistically rebuilding the world order remains to be seen, but the attempt itself is significant.

The Russian regime, too, has rejected dominant Western liberalism, but it has not articulated an ambitious project beyond a desire to reaffirm its military standing in the international arena.

Indeed, the way autocratic rule unfolds in China and Russia should be watched closely in the years to come as Xi introduces new political and economic policies during his limitless stay in power and Putin enters yet another six-year term.

While, thus far, the Chinese authoritarian model still features more participatory governance domestically and globally, this can change if Xi over-extends his personal ambitions at the cost of those of the Party, cuts out channels for public feedback, and embarks on a more aggressive foreign policy.

☐

THEIR POSITIVE IMPACTS

ON THEIR ECONOMIES

The positive impact of Putin and Xi Jinping on their economies has been profound during this time of uncertainty as they seek to position themselves as leaders on the global stage, achieving nothing short of what Franklin D. Roosevelt did in the aftermath of the Great Depression.

Good Things About Putin's Russia

The news out of Russia has mostly been bad — and deservedly so. Things have been going steadily downhill since the great protest march on the eve of President Vladimir Putin's third inauguration in May 2012.

But some perspectives has been lost in the process. There are good things about Putin's Russia as well. Here are the top 10:

1. You can leave. Andrei Sakharov, leader of the Human Rights movement in the Soviet Union, insisted that the No. 1 human right was the right to leave your country. Otherwise, you are living in a prison house. It is unfortunate that some people still have to flee Russia, but it is fortunate that they can.

Customer service has improved, there is less anti-Semitism, and Russians are free to pray and leave the country if they want.

2. You can pray. In my experience, it is a lot easier to find believers who are intelligent and fun in Russia than it is in the U.S. A Russian can be a member of the intellectual class and still follow the Orthodox Church's complex schedule of fasts. For all the cosy hypocrisy in the relations of church and state that the Pussy Riot punk rock group mocked in its prank at Moscow's main cathedral, it must still be counted as progress that believers can openly worship now without fearing social or economic loss as in Soviet times. That also raises the question of how long today's Russia should be compared to a Soviet yesterday.

3. You can open a business. What once were capital crimes are now career choices. The streets of some Russian cities now are now displaying more individual capitalism, the little stores with a personality that lend colour and variety to street-level life. Shopping is no longer an expedition. All sense of adventure has been lost. If you want something, you buy it — including on the Internet. E-commerce is a booming business in Russia. All you need is money, the new tyrant.

4. The Internet is free. My rule is that a country without free Internet can never be called free, whereas a country with a free Internet can never be called entirely unfree. The perverse irony here is that modern authoritarian regimes may actually prefer free Internet and social media because it makes it easier to track and monitor dissidents. Case in point: Protesters on the barricades in Kyiv received the following text message: "Dear subscriber, you are registered as a participant in an unsanctioned rally."

5. You can eat. When I used to travel to the Soviet hinterland, I always carried a salami, bread, and a knife. It was perfectly possible to end up in a town where there was no restaurant open and no food in the stores. Recently I had a few nice meals in Murmansk in the Arctic Circle. Everywhere you look, there are sushi restaurants, which somehow have become the emblem of modern dining sophistication — much like being pro-gay rights has become the emblem of the modern, civilized mindset. We'll know that Russia has arrived when we start seeing gay sushi restaurants popping up not only in Moscow but in the conservative hinterlands as well.

6. There is less anti-Semitism. Or maybe it has simply been exported to western Ukraine and Europe. In reality, of course, Russia's xenophobia and bile have been refocused on Central Asian guest workers and natives of the Caucasus. From time to time, you can see Orthodox Jews in black coats and hats, long beards, and pays walking down city streets un-self-consciously, lost in their own conversation and oblivious to the fact that they are in the country that gave the world the words "pogrom" and "Pale of Settlement."

I was amazed and gladdened when there was no detectable outbreak of anti-Semitism over the fact that so many of the oligarchs were Jewish. Of course, there is still some anti-Semitism in Russia, but perhaps only just enough to prove the old bitter maxim that anti-Semitism is hating Jews more than you should.

7. Weak commies. In a country once totally dominated by Communists, it is a pleasure to see them now as a mostly toothless opposition — often literally — whose existence helps keep up the appearances of tolerance and democracy. It also gives Westerners who remember the Cold War the opportunity to look at real Russian Communists who still sincerely believe all of that ideological claptrap. Their spectacular historical failure has now sent some Communists back to their original function: helping society's poor and forgotten.

8. Smiles and good service. In the bad old days, smiles were rare in general, and service was often called "unobtrusive" — meaning that the waiter or salesperson was nowhere to be found, having simply disappeared probably to stand in line for chicken or toilet paper. Service with a smile was outright inconceivable. Now Russians smile more often and more easily, and service is definitely speedier, probably because chicken and toilet paper are readily available in stores.

Nonetheless, you can still get the old-fashioned service with a scowl. On the bullet train between Moscow and St. Petersburg, the stewardesses are quick to bring you a surprisingly tasty lunch, but they slap it down on your tray and disappear to deal with things more important than customers, like gossip and makeup. The Soviet Union dies hard.

9. Alexei Navalny. It's wonderful that today's Russia could have a wise-cracking corruption-fighting whistle-blower like Navalny. He is a person of intelligence, integrity, and sufficient stature to worry Putin, especially after Navalny won an impressive 27 per cent of the vote in September's mayoral election in Moscow. There have already been efforts to cripple him with phoney criminal charges resulting in a conviction that may disbar him from any future political runs for office. There may even be efforts to crush him even more completely than that. At least he can leave the country — as of this writing, anyway.

10. Everything that always made Russia wonderful, no matter who rules from the Kremlin. The list includes vodka, jokes, excellent conversation, passionate friendship, vodka, heroic hospitality, banyas, a love of art and music, a sense of vastness reaching from steppe to space, and vodka.

How China Has Changed Under Xi Jinping

Xi Jinping emerged from the 20th Communist Party Congress with a precedent-breaking third leadership term, and a Politburo Standing Committee made up entirely of loyalists, cementing his place as China's most powerful ruler since Mao Zedong.

Under Xi's decade in power, China has undergone profound change, both domestically and within the global context.

Here are some of the ways that China has changed under Xi.

1. Perceptions of China in the West and U.S.-allied countries have worsened

U.S.-China relations have deteriorated sharply in recent years, a decline that accelerated under former U.S. President Donald Trump's hawkish turn on Beijing. But western perceptions also have been worsened by concerns over human rights as well as China's increasing aggression towards Taiwan.

2. Xi's campaign against corruption

Upon taking office, Xi initiated a signature drive to root out corruption within the Communist Party, which has proven popular with the public and which numerous analysts say has also been a useful tool for eliminating political opponents.

3. The taming of once-unruly borderlands

The regions of Tibet, Xinjiang, and Hong Kong, all far from Beijing, have long created headaches for China's ruling Communist Party.

Xi launched unprecedented, sweeping security crackdowns that brought the borderlands under control.

In Xinjiang, that included the internment of an estimated one million minority Muslim Uyghurs in camps; in Hong Kong, Beijing responded to major anti-government protests in 2019 with a sweeping national security law.

4. The state is increasingly taking the economic lead

Xi has ratcheted up state control and guidance of the economy, including a wide-ranging crackdown on the most free-wheeling sectors of the private sector, especially online platforms and for-profit education.

The clampdown on those sectors, as well as the impact of ongoing COVID-19 restrictions, has pushed up urban unemployment and pushed down consumer confidence.

5. Slowing growth, rising incomes

The era of double-digit yearly growth ended before Xi took office, and the rate of growth has been declining, which was inevitable as the size of the economy grows.

Incomes have steadily risen under Xi.

A growing number of analysts warn that China's investment-heavy, the infrastructure-driven model is increasingly unsustainable, with further slowdown ahead.

6. The uashing of dissent, the expansion of censorship

Xi has cracked down on domestic critics and protests, eliminating space for dissent, while censorship inside China's "Great Firewall" steadily intensifies.

7. The world's largest military grows, modernizes

The People's Liberation Army, led by Xi, has been closing the gap with the United States, including on the high seas, with major implications for tensions surrounding Taiwan, as China ratchets up its capability to seize the island on what some U.S. officials warn is a shortening timeline.

8. China leads in green tech — and pollution

While China struggles to shake its dependence on coal, it has become the global leader in the manufacture of electric vehicles and won plaudits for its pledge to achieve carbon neutrality by 2060. Most visibly, air quality in China has steadily improved over the past decade.

9. Extreme poverty is eliminated, but ineＱuality persists

Xi describes the elimination of extreme poverty in China as one of the key Communist Party achievements of the past decade.

IneＱuality, however, has proven a tougher challenge — especially the gap between urban and rural incomes — something Xi is seeking to tackle with his "common prosperity" policy.

China's official Gini coefficient numbers show that despite a slight decline in recent years, it still has one of the highest income ineＱualities among large economies, along with the United States.

THE ABSOLUTE POWERS OF VLADIMIR PUTIN AND XI JINPING

Putin's Absolute Power

Russia is a country with an autocratic form of government. This means that there is one leader, or dictator, who has absolute power over the country. President Vladimir Putin has been in power since 2000, and he controls every aspect of Russia's political system and society.

This is how Putin gains absolute power over Russia:

- Putin gains control over the media by controlling the ownership of television stations, newspapers, and studios.
- He also controls civil society by ordering raids on NGO offices and arresting members of opposition parties or volunteer groups to criminalize dissent.
- Putin governs Russia with a deep distrust of any information or organization that is not under his control.
- He controls the country with threats and violence, such as in Chechnya, where he killed over 50000 civilians.

- Putin also enforces censorship and suppresses the press by arresting journalists for publishing anything he does not approve of.

President Putin uses all of the these tactics to maintain absolute power. In such a country, human rights violations are common, elections are fixed, and government institutions are corrupt. The media is controlled by the government and social issues like poverty and unemployment are ignored by the government so that citizens will not dissent against it.

Xi Jinping's Chilling Grab For Absolute Power In China

The Xinhua news agency has just issued a long, unprecedented statement about directions from the Chinese Communist Party Central Committee to the National People's Congress regarding revisions to China's national constitution.

The People's Congress is now required to propose this revisions at its annual meeting next month.

If there was any doubt that China's national legislature is anything but a toothless rubber stamp for the secretive machinations of the Communist Politburo, there isn't anymore.

So it looks like President Xi Jinping, aged 64, and his proposed VP, Wang Qishan, 69, are in office for life. (Expect an approving tweet from Donald Trump, who must feel ever more resentful that he's buckled down by the United States comparable constitutional restriction.)

China's term limit was enacted in 1982 following a reassessment of the later years of Chairman Mao Zedong, who was the supreme leader from 1935 until his death in 1976.

The overwhelming consensus in China is that he stayed in power 20 years too long, with things going horribly wrong from 1957 with the large-scale purge of "rightists." This was followed by the disastrous Great Leap Forward economic campaign, which resulted in more than 30 million people dying of starvation. Then came to a decade of the massive destruction, upheaval, and political purges of the Cultural Revolution.

But at least Mao's power was somewhat constrained by colleagues like Zhou Enlai and Liu Shaoqi, who retained their own currency as leaders from the revolutionary wars.

Rivals vanⓆuished

By comparison, Xi Jinping has no such checks or balances, having already methodically purged potential rivals like Sun Zhengcai and Bo Xilai through anti-corruption campaigns. Xi has now assumed absolute control of the Party, Army, and state.

Only violence would dislodge him from power — some sort of extreme right-wing nationalist military coup that could bring a xenophobic expansionist régime even more hostile to Canadian interests than what we're facing now.

Any naive hopes for a peaceful evolution to democracy are shattered by the reality that China is now an one-man dictatorship yearning to restore the archaic political norms of China's imperial past: Subjects instead of citizens, the destiny of the nation instead of individuals' rights and protection of minority rights.

What's more, another of the constitutional revisions adds "Xi Jinping Thought on Socialism with Chinese Characteristics for a New Era" as the Party's ideological guide. In other words, whatever Xi says or does has the authority of supreme law in China.

As an one-time advisor in the Canadian embassy in Beijing, I believe the problem for Canada is that Xi has a fervent commitment to a meta-ideology that threatens the current, fraying liberal world order.

His **"Chinese dream of national restoration"** demands that Canada and all Western nations become subsidiary participants in the Chinese-dominated "community of the common destiny of humankind" linked by the massive "One Belt One Road" global infrastructure program.

Under a previous empire, all roads led to Rome. Under "Emperor" Xi, all high-speed rail lines under heaven, shipping routes (including via the Canadian Arctic), and air transport will pass through Beijing.

China is already aggressively rallying support from pro-mainland ethnic Chinese in Canada, as well as China-friendly business lobbyists and politicians, through its United Front Work Department initiatives in Canada.

If the political consensus in Canada is not to comply, expect China to retaliate. Britain, Australia, and New Zealand have already refused to support the One Belt One Road plan. They will certainly incur Beijing's wrath, starting with economic punishment as the stick and promise of trade and investment benefits for compliance with China's demands as the carrot.

The constitutional amendments also include new language about **"the great revival of the Chinese race."**

The threat to Chinese Canadians is that there is a much enhanced blood-and-belonging aspect to Xi's constitutionally endorsed rhetoric. This overarching vision sees all ethnic Chinese — regardless of citizenship or number of generations abroad, including even children adopted from China — as obligated to respond to Chinese Embassy pressures to facilitate China's rise through political support for Beijing and even treasonous espionage.

Canadians with family in China are pressured to demonstrate their loyalty to China's People's Republic. Canada must do much more to protect our countrymen of ethnic Chinese origin from foreign interference.

Under Xi Jinping's now unchallengeable dictatorship, the world is becoming more and more Chinese.

It's important that we make sure this doesn't mean that Canada has to become less and less Canadian.

THEIR NEGATIVE IMPACTS ON THEIR ECONOMIES

It's no secret that Vladimir Putin and Xi Jinping are two of the most powerful men in the world. What is a bit of a secret, however, is what effect their leadership has had on their respective countries. Read on to understand some of the bad and corrupt things they have respectively did in their countries

Corruption In The Xi Jinping Era

Since the opening up of the Chinese economy by Deng Xiaoping in 1979, China has grown wealthy, but corruption has also become pervasive at all levels of the Chinese Communist Party (CCP). Corruption has been a part of Chinese business and governance for millennia, but despite the grand pronouncements of the CCP about eradicating corruption, it has not only endured under the current system but has grown to extraordinary heights. Due to deeply entrenched corruption across the government, as well as the variable spread of economic benefits, this issue will remain a severe challenge for the CCP as the Xi Jinping era enters its second decade. The necessity for the state security agencies to support political control Xi will also ensure that anti-corruption purges continue to impact the police and security agencies.

Purges Continue

In July, former Deputy Minister of Public Security Fu Zhenghua pleaded guilty in the Changchun Intermediate People's Court in Jilin Province to charges of bribery relating to 117 million yuan ($17 million) and abuse of power from 2005 to 2021. Fu's alleged corruption occurred during his tenure as Director of the Beijing Public Security Bureau (PSB) and later as Deputy Minister of Public Security, which involved oversight of policing across the People's Republic of China (PRC) (South China Morning Post (SCMP), July 29).

The arrest and conviction of Fu is part of a prolonged crackdown on corrupt officials during Xi Jinping's tenure, which from early 2021 onward, has focused on law enforcement agencies. The scale and extent of the crackdown indicate that policing in China may be endemically corrupt. The CCP aggressively pursued corruption that grew during the high economic growth years after 1979, which affected all arms of government but especially the PSB, as its officers have been poorly, paid, with many consequently resorting to illegitimate means to benefit from the increasing wealth in China.

However, the continued arrests of senior officers indicate that Xi and his faction in the CCP intend to secure the loyalty of the PSB and other security agencies by using anti-corruption as a tool of control. The complete obedience of the PSB to the CCP and their reliability to implement restrictive social controls is an essential part of China's expanding police state that undergirds one-party rule. Corruption in the PSB at both junior and senior levels weakens public trust in policing and, as a result, undermines the rule of the CCP in the police state.

Several recent corruption cases also involve action taken against officers who were members of political factions that may have posed a potential threat to President Xi and his clique of supporters, such as those associated with former CCP leaders Bo Xilai and Zhou Yongkang (China Brief, October 14, 2021). This has led to the purge of a large number of senior officials in the public security system and some in the state security bureaucracy, which may have been more about political loyalty than corruption. The aim of such a purge is to ensure obedience and fear amongst public security officials so that the security apparatus can be controlled by President Xi without fear of a challenge. However, these cases indicate that the individuals, as well as possible political threats, were also deeply corrupt.

The PSB and the Party

PSBs at national, provincial, and municipal levels maintain public order, enforce all criminal laws, also have some responsibilities for national security, and, as a result, have a huge amount of power as the primary means by which the CCP exerts control over citizens. This control flows down from the national to local levels through the Ministry of Public Security (MPS), which coordinates the work of the provincial and municipal PSBs, although they report directly to local leaders who have a great deal of autonomy and, conse🄯uently, an opportunity for misconduct.

The MPS has a policing role but also serves political security and counterintelligence functions. The MPS was created in 1949 with the abolishment of the Social Affairs Department of the Central Committee of the CCP and the absorption of its personnel. This enabled the move of public security functions from the Party to the state, although the leadership at that time was drawn from the ranks of the People's Liberation Army (PLA), either generals or political commissars, and the military maintained strong control or influence over the MPS up until the late 1970s.

Although the MPS was separated from the CCP structure, it remained a tool of the Party under Mao Zedong and was essential to the survival of high-ranking CCP leaders during periods of instability. During the Cultural Revolution, eight MPS Vice Ministers were arrested, suspended, or dismissed. In September 1966, PLA representatives took charge of the MPS using military force to impose control, and most of the former national, provincial and local police leaders were sent to CCP schools and labour camps for education. Only after Deng Xiaoping started to implement reforms in 1975 were PLA officers gradually moved out of MPS leadership.

The reforms started by Deng did not really separate the Party and state in the MPS bureaucracy, which, like all organs of the PRC state, involved the Party having indirect influence over the policing and security agencies. PSB offices at the provincial and municipal level have leaders with multiple governments and CCP roles, such as membership of local Party committees, which have an important role in police recruitment, promotion, salary, and benefits, as well as resource allocation. Despite the formal separation, the Party has controlled the PSB since the creation of the MPS in 1949. As the Party controls the MPS, the influence of the CCP Secretary General (who is also the President) is paramount.

The PSB, Politics, and Corruption

The large number of cases involving senior officers indicates that corruption in the PSB may be endemic. For so many cases at such senior levels, involving networks of police officers across different provinces, to occur over such a prolonged period of time suggests that corruption is not confined to isolated "bad apples" but has become widespread across the PSB.

In January, Sun Lijun, Vice Minister of Public Security, pleaded guilty to charges of accepting bribes of 646 million yuan ($95 million), manipulating the securities market, and illegally holding firearms (Caixin, January 14). Sun began his police career in 1988, and in 2018 became the youngest Deputy Minister of the MPS, where he was in charge of the First Bureau responsible for domestic security in the PRC, including in Hong Kong and Macau, and was also part of a team sent to Wuhan at the start of the COVID-19 epidemic (SCMP, July 8). For, a senior officer with such sensitive responsibilities to be convicted of corruption is an extraordinary indictment of the system that allowed him to be promoted to such a level.

Other senior officers were implicated in the "Sun faction." In September 2021, Wang Like, former Director of the PSB and Secretary of the Politics and Legal Affairs Commission of the Jiangsu Provincial Committee, was dismissed from public office and expelled from the CCP for disloyalty, bribery, and several other corruption-related allegations, with his case transferred to the prosecutorial authorities (Central Commission for Discipline Inspection, September 22, 2021). Wang started his police career in the 1980s in Liaoning Province, where he worked with Wang Lijun, who was later Director of the PSB in Chong️ing Municipality and, in 2012, was convicted of corruption, attempted defection, as well as involvement in the murder of a British businessman Neil Heywood (Creaders.net, October 15, 2012). The indications of the political reason for the prosecution of Wang Like come from his association with Wang Lijun, who reported to former CCP Secretary of Chong☐ing Bo Xilai, once considered to have been a political rival of Xi Jinping, but who was purged a decade ago and is currently serving a lifetime prison sentence.

Also implicated in the crackdown on the "Sun faction" were former PSB directors Deng Huilin of Chongqing, Gong Doan of Shanghai, and Liu Xinyun of Shanxi province (Caixin, January 17). Reports of these investigations, arrests, and convictions indicate a web of nepotism and corruption that stretched across multiple provinces at the highest levels of the PSB's leadership.

Deng Huilin, the successor of Wang Lijun as Director of the Chong☐ing PSB, was removed from office in January 2021 and accused of using his post to seek profit for others, illegally accepting property, speaking ill of government policies, and engaging in superstitious activities (China Daily, January 4, 2021). Deng pleaded guilty to bribery charges during his trial at the People's Court of Baoding City in Hebei Province (China.org.cn, September 11, 2021).

Gong Doan, Deputy Mayor of Shanghai and Director of the PSB, was arrested in April 2020 and later charged with abuse of power, corruption, misconduct, and building cliｑues within the Party (SCMP, February 11, 2021).

Liu Xinyun, the former Deputy Governor of Shanxi Province and Director of the Shanxi Public Security Department, was removed from his position in April 2021 for corruption. Liu was previously head of cyber operations at the MPS in Beijing and led the PRC's implementation of big data, Internet monitoring, and other technologies for policing (SCMP, April 12, 2021). In January, Liu was charged at the Langfang Intermediate Court in Hebei Province with taking advantage of his various posts to assist companies and individuals with business operations in return for accepting cash and gifts worth over 13.3 million yuan ($2.09 million) between 1998 and 2021 (China Daily, January 6).

The cases against the "Sun faction" of Deng, Gong, and Liu illustrated that the purge is not only about eradicating corruption but also about eliminating threats from "cliques" that, if not broken, could develop inappropriate levels of political influence. A CCTV documentary on the "Sun faction" noted that "In Sun Lijun's values, grabbing greater political power and obtaining greater economic benefits are two inseparable aspects." (Central Commission for Discipline Inspection, January 15)

The convictions of Sun Lijun and others in the "Sun faction" were preceded in 2018 by the arrest of Meng Hongwei, who was President of INTERPOL in 2016 and previously served as Vice Minister of Public Security in China as well as Director of the Coast Guard. This case was a far higher profile episode than the domestic PSB arrests, as Meng was in charge of INTERPOL. Meng confessed to the charges against him in the First Intermediate People's Court of Tianjin and was sentenced to thirteen and a half years of imprisonment. Meng admitted to accepting bribes totalling 14.46 million yuan ($2.14 million) between 2005 and 2017 (Global Times, June 20, 2019).

There are also indications of political infighting in Meng's case. Chen Yixin, Secretary-General of the Commission for Political and Legal Affairs of the CCP Central Committee, is reported to have written that Meng Hongwei, Wang Like, Gong Doan, Deng Huiling, and Sun Lijun were all "two-faced persons" who seriously violated party discipline (Global Times, October 2, 2021). However, Grace Weng, the wife of Meng Hongwei, said in an interview that the case against her husband was "an example of a political disagreement being turned into a criminal affair" (AP, November 18, 2021).

Some Of The Bad And Corrupt Things
Putin Has Done

Is the U.N. really just a club of rich nations, and is the world falling apart? Let's see what some of the bad and corrupt things Putin has done.

1) In 2002, Putin pushed through legislation that made it illegal for advocacy groups like Amnesty International, Human Rights Watch, and Greenpeace to operate in Russia. In 2014, these organizations were banned from performing any activities at all in Russia due to an updated law. These groups have had major issues with freedom of expression and were providing critical news about human rights violations in Russia (such as, according to Amnesty International). With the new law, they can be subject to fines of up to $50,000. Vladimir Putin has also said that the ban was made so that Russia would be in full compliance with international law and not exposed to lawsuits.

2) Russian intelligence agents interfered in the 2016 U.S. election. In fact, one of their main goals was to secure a victory for Donald Trump over Hillary Clinton! Wikileaks founder Julian Assange boldly admitted as much in an interview: "We knew ... that at least some of our publications were going to be picked up by Raw Story because we had our own separate database, and so I'm sure that

there are thousands of other examples just like this. We have direct knowledge of the Russian government polling voters, feeding false information to these online media."

3) Russia has also been accused of hacking into the private emails of Hillary Clinton and the Democratic National Committee. Some claim that it was directly because Putin wanted to get Donald Trump, but honestly, how could he have known what Hillary or the DNC were going to do? They were hacked shortly before they released their emails. Some experts even claim that they hacked into their computers, but then when they found out that they were not being kept secure enough (as Hillary was worried about), so they simply deleted all that info! Mind-bogglingly stupid.

4) Critics have accused Putin, who was once an officer of the KGB and intelligence services, of using these tactics to craft a complex system, totally controlled by him, for the purpose of biasing elections, manipulating information and public opinion, punishing dissidents, and enriching his own friends.

5) One thing that Putin did in response to this was to fund the "Internet Research Agency," which is basically similar to Russia's infamous troll factories! It is located in Saint Petersburg and has a monthly budget of $1.2 million! (The equivalent of several

thousand dollars per months per employee.) In fact, they even had usernames that were identical or virtually identical to actual Americans and/or soon-to-be Trump supporters. They would then post political comments and memes on social media such as Twitter and Facebook. These groups and sites are often called "troll farms."

6) The other thing that he did to help try to influence the election was to fund far-right European political parties! They have been accused of helping in the Brexit vote too! Many people do not realize that Britain's vote for leaving the European Union (aka Brexit) was incredibly close, with just under 52% voting to leave and 48% voting to stay. And if you look into who supported Brexit, it was primarily older voters in less economically developed regions of England and Wales or those with low levels of education. It was also a younger, more educated population in London and Scotland that voted to stay.

7) Putin has also used the state-controlled media to boost Russian nationalism, or Russophilia, using negative portrayals of NATO, the West, and the U.S., and portraying NATO as an "aggressor" while reframing Russia's own regional conflicts as defensive measures. This was done according to leaked cables from the U.S. embassy in Moscow, which spoke of a "strategy of tension" that built up animosity against western nations towards Russia.

8) Putin has also been accused of putting Russian nuclear weapons on high alert! This was done in response to NATO's deployment of the ballistic missile defence system in Europe: "According to a former U.S. official, Putin had concluded that an attack on Russia was 'more likely than not,' and raised Russian strategic nuclear forces to the highest level since the early 1980s."

9) In truth, Putin is a much worse dictator than Trump! I know some people won't agree with me, but here are six reasons why:

- He has been accused of murdering journalists.
- He actively works to silence media outlets by using intimidation and purchasing them out.
- He has pushed through legislation that makes it illegal for advocacy groups like Amnesty International, Human Rights Watch, and Greenpeace to operate in Russia. 4) One of his primary goals is to interfere with the U.S. election.
- He has even been accused of interfering with the Brexit vote!
- And finally, he regularly uses the state-controlled media to boost Russian nationalism and even put nuclear weapons on high alert!

The truth is that Putin is a strong leader who doesn't let his people forget how much they mean to him. His main goal is to increase his own power and stay in power, and this often requires cracking down on democracy. Add the fact that he is old, has even been accused of murdering journalists, and is incredibly paranoid, working to silence media outlets with intimidation in an attempt to get them to speak badly about him, and you have a man who is worse than Trump.

I don't think Trump cares about most people in the world. But he's not our enemy. I wish there was some way we could work with him or at least understand him.

STRATEGIC INTERACTION AND SPRING VISIT: PUTIN AND XI JINPING

MOSCOW, December 30. /TASS/. Relations between Moscow and Beijing have withstood all tests and are a model of cooperation between major powers in the 21st century, Russian President Vladimir Putin said during a conversation with Chinese President Xi Jinping by video link on Friday.

The Russian leader also said that he looks forward to his Chinese counterpart's visit to Moscow in the spring, and the latter assured him of Beijing's readiness to increase strategic cooperation with its neighbour and "be global partners."

TASS collected the main theses from the open part of the talks, which were the first for the two leaders since Xi Jinping was re-elected as General Secretary of the Communist Party of China Central Committee in October.

On Russian-Chinese Partnership

"In the context of soaring geopolitical tensions, the importance of the Russian-Chinese strategic partnership as a stabilizing force is growing," Putin said, noting that relations between the two countries demonstrated maturity and stability and continued to expand "dynamically", and they are "the best in history."

Moscow and Beijing share the same views on the causes and course of the transformation of the geopolitical landscape. Putin emphasized that Russia and China are defending their positions of principle while protecting the interests of both of their nations and all those who advocate for truly democratic world order and the right of countries to freely determine their fate.

The Chinese President also stressed the close strategic contract with the Russian President: "Under our joint leadership, the Chinese-Russian comprehensive partnership and strategic interaction in the new era demonstrate resistance to stress."

Xi Jinping also assured Putin that China, "in the face of a simple and far from the unambiguous international situation," is ready to "increase strategic cooperation with Russia, provide each other with development opportunities, and be global partners."

About Xi Jinping's Visit

The Chinese President is expected to pay a state visit to Moscow next spring.

"I have no doubt that we will find an opportunity to meet in person," Putin said.

He stressed that this visit "will show the strength of Russian-Chinese ties on key issues to the world and will become the main political event of the year in bilateral relations."

The last time the Presidents of Russia and China met in person in a bilateral format was on the sidelines of the Shanghai Cooperation Organization summit in mid-September. In early February, Putin flew to Beijing, where he held talks with Xi Jinping.

On Trade And Gas

Trade turnover between Russia and China is growing at a record-high pace and will increase. "Despite the unfavourable external environment, illegitimate restrictions, and certain Western countries' direct blackmail, Russia and China managed to ensure record high rates of mutual trade turnover growth," the Russian President said. Trade turnover "rose by around 25%," he noted, adding that such dynamics would enable the two countries "to reach the targeted level of $200 bln by 2024."

The President also noted the unprecedented volumes of exports of Russian hydrocarbons to China: as for pipeline gas supplies, Russia ranks second, and in terms of liquefied natural gas supplies, it is in fourth place. Moscow will increase supplies next year, Putin assured.

The Russian leader also recalled the implementation of landmark infrastructure projects - for example, in the outgoing year, for the first time in the history of bilateral relations, permanent automobile and railway bridges appeared on the Amur border river.

About Military Cooperation

Military and military-technical cooperation between the two countries contributes not only to ensure their own security but also to "maintaining stability in key regions," Putin said. He added that Moscow intends to strengthen cooperation with Beijing in this area.

Summing Up The Year's Results

Putin called Xi Jinping a dear friend and noted "a very good tradition" to talk via video link at the end of the year - "to sum up the results of work and outline plans <...>, to exchange views on the most pressing international issues."

Last year, the President of Russia and the President of China had such a conversation on December 15, and on December 30, Putin called up another world leader - U.S. President Joe Biden. The main topic of that conversation was Russia's demands for security guarantees, the unsatisfactory state of relations between Moscow and Washington, as well as the situation around Ukraine. Biden then expressed concern about the movement of troops near the Ukrainian border and threatened sanctions in the event of an escalation.

XI AND PUTIN URGE NATO TO RULE OUT EXPANSION AS UKRAINE TENSIONS RISE

China's Xi Jinping and Vladimir Putin of Russia have signed a joint statement calling on the West to "abandon the ideologized approaches of the cold war" as the two leaders showcased their warming relationship in Beijing at the start of the Winter Olympics.

The politicians also said the bonds between the two countries had "no limits." "There is no 'forbidden' areas of cooperation,'" they declared.

In the joint statement released by the Kremlin, Putin, and Xi called on Nato to rule out expansion in eastern Europe, denounced the formation of security blocs in the Asia Pacific region, and criticized the Aukus trilateral security pact between the U.S., U.K. and Australia.

The two leaders met for the 38th time since 2013. The two countries also pledged to step up cooperation to thwart "colour revolutions" and external interference and vowed to further deepen "back-to-back" strategic coordination.

The statement declared that the new Sino-Russia relations were "superior to political and military alliances of the cold war era." It shows the ambitions and anxieties China and Russia both share and how they have increasingly found a common interest in their respective disagreements with western powers, analysts say.

"The parties oppose the further expansion of Nato, call on the North Atlantic alliance to abandon the ideologized approaches of the cold war, respect the sovereignty, security, and interests of other countries, the diversity of their civilizational and cultural-historical patterns, and treat the peaceful development of other states objectively and fairly," the document said.

In a nod to Russian interests in Ukraine, China said it "understands and supports the proposals put forward by the Russian Federation on the formation of long-term legally binding security guarantees in Europe," the document said.

At the same time, it addressed Chinese concerns about US-led trade and security alliances in its own region – something Beijing has intensified its criticism of in recent years.

"The parties oppose the formation of closed bloc structures and opposing camps in the Asia Pacific region and remain highly vigilant about the negative impact of the U.S. Indo-Pacific strategy on peace and stability in this region," it read.

While there are still stumbling blocks in the relationship and a fully-fledged alliance between Moscow and Beijing is unlikely, the two sides are signalling that they want to roll back U.S. influence in their respective regions.

"We are working together to bring to life true multilateralism," Xi told Putin, according to the Kremlin translation of their remarks. "Defending the real spirit of democracy serves as a reliable foundation for uniting the world in overcoming crises and defending equality."

The statement also devoted an entire section to the two sides' shared understanding of "democracy" and claimed both countries "have long-standing traditions of democracy." But they said that the advocacy of democracy and human rights "must not be used to put pressure on other countries."

Friday's meeting was Xi's first face-to-face engagement with a foreign leader in nearly two years. The Chinese leader had not left the country since January 2020, when it was grappling with its initial Covid-19 outbreak and locked down the central city of Wuhan, where the virus was first reported.

He is preparing to meet more than 20 leaders as Beijing kicks off a Winter Olympics it hopes will be a soft-power triumph and shift focus away from a buildup blighted by a diplomatic boycott and Covid fears.

It was also a rare trip abroad for Putin, who has left Russia just twice since the outbreak of Covid-19 and has maintained a healthy distance from visiting leaders such as Hungary's Viktor Orbán.

But as he strode toward Xi on Friday, Putin gave a wide smile and shook the Chinese leader's hand before posing for photographers. The two are expected to attend the Olympic opening ceremony on Friday evening.

Following their talks, Russia and China also, signed a series of trade and energy deals, including a new contract for Russia to supply an additional 10bn cubic meters of gas each year to China, Putin announced. Gazprom announced the 30-year contract to deliver the gas from Russia's far east to the Chinese state energy corporation CNPC, Reuters reported.

Russia already supplies China with about 38bn cubic meters of gas each year via its Power of Siberia pipeline and is eyeing a second pipeline that would open an additional market for Yamal peninsula gas fields as its Nord Stream 2 pipeline to Germany has been threatened with sanctions in case of a Russian attack on Ukraine.

The leaders of both France and Germany have said they plan to travel to Moscow in the coming weeks to continue talks with Putin and head off a potential invasion of Ukraine. The French President, Emmanuel Macron, is expected to visit Moscow on Monday and then travel to Kyiv on Tuesday as he practices shuttle diplomacy between Putin and the Ukrainian President, Volodymyr Zelensky. Germany's Olaf Scholz will travel to Kyiv on the February 14 and Moscow the next day.

China's state-run Xinhua news agency also carried an article from Putin on Thursday in which the Russian leader painted a portrait of two neighbours with increasingly shared global goals.

"Foreign policy coordination between Russia and China are based on close and coinciding approaches to solving global and regional issues," Putin wrote.

He also hit out at US-led diplomatic boycotts of the Beijing Olympics that were sparked by China's human rights record.

"Sadly, attempts by a number of countries to politicize sports for their selfish interests have recently intensified," Putin wrote, calling such moves "fundamentally wrong."

For it's part, China has become more vocal in backing Russia in its dispute with Nato powers over Ukraine.

Moscow is looking for support after its deployment of 100,000 troops near its border with Ukraine prompted western nations to warn of an invasion and threaten "severe conse?uences" in response to any Russian attack.

China enjoyed plentiful support from the Soviet Union – the precursor to the modern Russian state – after the establishment of Communist rule in 1949, but the two socialist powers later fell out over ideological differences.

Vladimir Putin with the head of FSB director Alexander Bortnikov (right) and other officials on Security Services Day in Moscow in 2015.

Putin's Security Men: The Elite Group Who 'Fuel His Anxieties.'

Relations got back on track as the cold war ended in the 1990s, and the pair have pursued a strategic partnership in recent years that has seen them work closely on trade, military, and geopolitical issues.

Those bonds have strengthened further during the Xi Jinping era, at a time when Russia and China find themselves increasingly at odds with western powers. In 2014, in a show of defiance against fierce western criticism over the annexation of Crimea, Putin turned to Xi to look for an alternative. Beijing showed its support by signing a $400bn, 30-year gas deal.

Other leaders set to enjoy Xi's hospitality during the Games include Egypt's Abdel Fatah al-Sisi, Saudi Arabia's Mohammed bin Salman, Kassym-Jomart Tokayev of Kazakhstan, and Poland's Andrzej Duda.

About 21 world leaders are expected to attend the Games. A majority of those leaders rule non-democratic regimes, according to the Economist Intelligence Unit's Democracy Index, with 12 labelled either "authoritarian" or a "hybrid regime."

CONCLUSION

Obviously, the West still doesn't really understand Putin's personality. For U.S. think tanks, which once housed so many experts on the USSR, it's much easier to study the Communist Party than to research Putin's personality. The Communist Party has principles that are different from the West's, but it does have principles. By contrast, Putin is relying on his personality, not principles, to govern Russia. This personality is shaped by his education, his personal experiences, and his understanding of Russia and its people. The West may not like Putin, but what Western leaders can say they understand Russia better than Putin does?

When I told my American friend that, in Xi Jinping, China had another Putin rather than a Gorbachev or a Yeltsin, he was somewhat disappointed. After a pause, he sighed and said to me," Putin is not that popular." I said that was the viewpoint of Western people. In Russia, Putin is obviously more popular than Gorbachev or Yeltsin. My friend then asked me if I liked Putin. I immediately replied, "We are not talking about my personal preference. We are talking about the current situation in Russia."

Putin's ruling Russia as a strongman seems to have resolved many of the problems left over from the Yeltsin era, which were problems common to many emerging democracies. But eventually, Russia will have to pay the price for backsliding on human rights and values. As the saying goes, what goes around comes around.

The problem for Russia is exactly that Putin is a strongman: within Putin's political Party, he's the only person who can fill that role. This means Putin's "strongman government" has an obvious personal flavour. For Putin, he can hold onto power as long as he lives, but for a politician (especially an ambitious politician), this isn't enough. After suffering the troubled decade of Yeltsin's democratic transformation, Putin has temporarily brought Russia back to the authoritarian era based on his understanding of Russia's national conditions. But can Putin use his strongman government to initiate orderly economic and social development? When the time is right, can he strike a balance between economic growth and democratic development, between a rising standard of living and democracy, and between personal freedom and political freedom?

Right now, Russia's's future hinges on Putin's will. He could hold onto power for the next decade to maintain Russia's national stability and great power status and continue to develop the economy even while beginning a new era of democratic diversity. Or Putin could take holding on to power as his only goal, not caring about what will happen to Russia after his death. Obviously, Russia will be lucky if Putin chooses the former. In the case of the latter choice, Russia will be in for some hard times.

Printed in Great Britain
by Amazon

41621852R00040